Shaping Books
41 Theme-Based Publishing Projects

by Cynthia G. Holzschuher

Fearon Teachers Aids
A Division of Frank Schaffer Publications

Editors: Susan Eddy
Cover and inside design: Deborah Walkoczy
Cover photograph: John Paul Endress

Fearon Teacher Aids
A Division of Frank Schaffer Publications, Inc.
23740 Hawthorne Boulevard
Torrance, CA 90505-5927

This Fearon Teacher Aids product was formerly manufactured and
distributed by American Teaching Aids, Inc., a subsidiary of Silver Burdett
Ginn, and is now manufactured and distributed by Frank Schaffer
Publications, Inc. FEARON, FEARON TEACHER AIDS, and the FEARON
balloon logo are marks used under license from Simon & Schuster, Inc.

ISBN 1-56417-683-5

 3 4 5 6 7 8 9 MAL 05 04 03 02 01 00 99

Contents

Shaping Books contains directions and patterns for 41 thematic book-jacket projects–innovative and creative ideas for making books with children. Using readily available materials and following simple directions, children may work individually, in small groups, or as a class to create these engaging projects.

Some of the projects result in books in which the text may be predetermined by you and copied by children. Others allow for children's original stories, poems, riddles, or other creations. Books such as these provide wonderful culminating activities for any writing assignment as well as a sense of ownership and accomplishment for the authors. Encourage children to work through the entire publishing process (prewrite, draft, revise, edit, publish) before transferring their original stories into finished books. Suggest that children keep a library of their original books, and be sure to display the books lavishly in your classroom library as well.

You may wish to create a publishing center in your room, where three or four students can work to create their books with help from a parent or aide or by following rebus charts you or a volunteer create. Or, instead of charts, you might like to make a set of partially assembled books that sequentially demonstrate each step of the directions. Whatever you provide, *be sure to demonstrate the steps for assembling each book before students attempt to make their own.* It will be necessary for you to precut paper or tagboard in some cases, such as the cage book for an animal theme. The abilities of your children will determine whether they trace and cut out the various shapes using the patterns provided or whether you do. Be sure to provide a place for students to store unfinished work in folders. You will need the following supplies in your publishing center.

- **colored construction paper**
- **white drawing paper**
- **crayons or markers**
- **stapler**
- **scissors**
- **yarn or ribbon**
- **brass fasteners**
- **masking tape**

- **colored tagboard**
- **ruled writing paper**
- **pencils**
- **hole punch**
- **rulers**
- **metal rings**
- **pipe cleaners**
- **glue sticks**

Book With Moveable Self-Character

This is a great project for the beginning of the school year. Invite students to read their books aloud to each other as a "getting-to-know-you" activity.

Materials (for each book)

- **2 sheets of tagboard, 9 in. x 12 in. (22.5 cm x 30 cm) each**
- **scissors**
- **masking tape**
- **pattern on page 49**
- **1 tagboard scrap for child cutout, 3 in. x 6 in. (7.5 cm x 15 cm)**
- **crayons or markers**
- **hole punch**
- **1 piece of yarn or string, 18 in. (45 cm)**
- **pencil**
- **lined writing paper**
- **stapler**

Directions

1. To make the front cover, cut a 1-inch strip from the 9-inch side of one piece of tagboard. Turn the tagboard over and reattach the strip along the entire length with masking tape. The tape should be on the inside of the cover. This creates a hinge for easy opening. The other piece of tagboard will be the back cover.

2. Using the pattern, trace the outline of a child on a scrap of tagboard. Color the child to look like you. Cut around the shape. Punch a hole in the right shoulder. Thread one end of the yarn through the hole and tie a knot. Set aside.

3. Decorate the cover with pictures of things you love. Print the title "All About Me." Cut a slot in the cover to hold your tagboard character. You may wish to make special decorations around this slot.

4. Write a story about yourself and your family. Put the pages in order and staple inside the covers. Punch a hole in the upper-left corner of the cover.

5. Attach your character to the cover by tying the loose end of yarn securely to the hole in the front cover. Tuck the character in the slot so that it peeks out.

Cage Book

During an animal, zoo, or circus unit, invite children to write about favorite zoo animals or visits to the circus or zoo.

Materials (for each book)

- **2 squares of colored tagboard, 8 in. (20 cm) each**
- **scissors**
- **masking tape**
- **hole punch**
- **3 pipe cleaners**
- **crayons or markers**
- **1 square of white drawing paper, 8 in. (20 cm)**
- **pencil**
- **several square sheets white writing paper, 8 in. (20 cm) each**
- **stapler**

Directions

1. To make the front cover, cut a 1-inch strip from one side of one piece of tagboard. Turn the tagboard over and reattach the strip along the entire length with masking tape. The tape should be on the inside of the cover. This creates a hinge for easy opening. The other piece of tagboard will be the back cover.

2. Cut a 5-inch (12.5-cm) square from the center of the front cover.

3. Punch three holes across the top and bottom of the front-cover opening. Attach three pipe cleaners for bars.

4. Draw a picture of your favorite animal in the center of the drawing paper.

5. On the writing paper, write a story about the animal.

6. Assemble the finished pages in order and staple them between the covers.

Book With Split Pages

This is a terrific project to help kids understand the concept of opposites. You can also use it for synonyms, homophones, or for contractions with older children.

Materials (for each book)

- **1 sheet colored construction paper, 9 in. x 12 in. (22.5 x 30 cm)**
- **3–4 sheets white drawing paper, 9 in. x 12 in. (22.5 x 30 cm)**
- **stapler**
- **ruler**
- **pencil**
- **scissors**
- **crayons or markers**

Directions

1. Fold the construction paper in half to make a 6-inch x 9-inch (22.5 cm x 15 cm) cover. Write *Antonyms* on the cover.

2. Stack the white drawing paper and fold it in half to make 6-inch x 9-inch pages.

3. Slip the pages inside the cover. Staple near the left edge.

4. Using a ruler, measure and mark the center of the first page with a horizontal line. Cut through all the pages by cutting along this center line. Stop near the stapled edge—do not cut all the way through. You now have "top" pages and "bottom" pages.

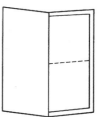

5. Decide on several antonyms to illustrate. Print one of the word pairs on the first top right-hand page and draw a picture of it. Turn the bottom page only. Print the word's opposite on the bottom left-hand page so that it cannot be seen immediately when opening to the first pair word.

6. Continue in this way until the book illustrates several antonyms.

Apple-Shaped Pop-up Booklet

Here's a cute autumn project that has no spooks or goblins. Young children may need some help with the folding.

Materials (for each booklet)

- **apple pattern on page 50 reproduced on red or yellow copier or construction paper**
- **scissors**
- **pencil**
- **crayons or markers**

Directions

1. Cut out the apple booklet on the solid lines.

2. Print an apple-related story on the writing lines. Add an illustration at the bottom of the page.

3. Follow the directions for folding so that the side sections fold into the center. Get some help from a grown-up if you need it.

4. Decorate the front of the apple and add a title.

Picture-Frame Book

This makes a nice tie-in to a discussion of a famous artist. Vincent Van Gogh, Winslow Homer, and Andrew Wyeth are among many students' favorites.

Materials (for each book)

- **2 squares of colored tagboard, 8 1/2 in. (20 cm) each**
- **masking tape**
- **1 square white drawing paper, 8 1/2 in. (20 cm)**
- **1 square lined writing paper, 8 1/2 in. (20 cm)**
- **scissors**
- **crayons or markers**
- **watercolors (optional)**
- **pencil**
- **stapler**

Directions

1. To make the front cover, cut a 1-inch strip from the side of one piece of tagboard. Turn the tagboard over and reattach the strip down the entire length with masking tape. The tape should be on the inside of the cover. This creates a hinge for easy opening. This book may open from the bottom or from the right.

2. Cut a 5-inch (12.5-cm) square from the center of the cover. Decorate the border like a picture frame. Laminate for durability and to create "glass" in the frame.

3. Draw or paint a picture on the white drawing paper that will show through the frame opening.

4. Write a descriptive paragraph about your drawing on the writing paper.

5. Assemble the pages in order and staple them to the cover near the left-hand side or top—wherever you have placed the hinge.

Backpack Book

This is a more involved project that perhaps is better suited to older children. Young children will love the results, however, if they can get some assistance putting it all together.

Materials (for each book)

- **pattern on page 51**
- **scissors**
- **1 sheet of red construction paper, 9 in. x 12 in. (22.5 cm x 30 cm)**
- **1 strip of red construction paper, 1/2 in. x 12 in. (1.5 cm x 30 cm)**
- **1 piece of red construction paper, 4 in. x 2 in. (10 cm x 5 cm)**
- **construction paper and writing paper to make small books**
- **stapler**
- **black marker or crayon**
- **glue stick**

Directions

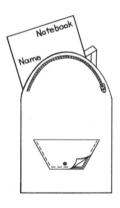
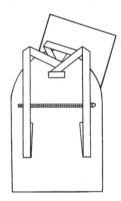

1. Use the pattern to trace and cut out the backpack shape from the sheet of red construction paper. Fold on the center dotted line. Draw the zipper indicated on the pattern and cut carefully along the line.

2. Cut a flap for the front using the pattern and the piece of red construction paper. Cut writing pages from white paper using the same pattern. Staple in place on the backpack. List your school supplies in the minibook.

3. Draw a zipper on the front of the backpack along the top edge.

4. Seal the bottom and side with a glue stick, leaving the top curve open.

5. Cut the narrow strip of construction paper in half to make two straps and glue or staple in place.

6. Make several small books with construction-paper covers that will fit inside your backpack.

Crayon-Box Book

Precutting the pages for this book provides a wonderful sequencing and color-word project for young children.

Materials (for each book)

- **8 copies of the pattern on p. 52, cut to show from one to eight crayons**
- **2 sheets of yellow construction paper, 7 1/2 in. x 9 in.**

  (18 cm x 22.5 cm)
- **crayons**
- **scissors**
- **stapler**

Directions

1. Arrange the book pages so that the one-crayon page is on top, the two-crayon page is underneath, and so on until the eight-crayon page is on the bottom. Staple the eight pages together along the left edge.

2. Color the crayon tips red, blue, yellow, orange, green, purple, brown, and black. Print the correct color words on each crayon.

3. Add a small illustration to go with each color, such as an apple for red.

4. Add yellow construction-paper covers. Decorate the front cover to resemble a crayon box. Sign your name in the lower right-hand corner.

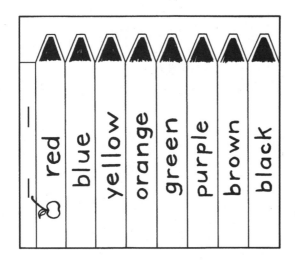

Pencil Accordion Book

If the crayon box book on page 13 seems too young for your students' first day of school, try this project, which provides more space for creative writing.

Materials (for each book)

- **1 sheet of yellow construction paper**
- **pattern on page 49**
- **1 sheet of writing or drawing paper, 6 in. x 11 in. (17.5 cm x 27.5 cm)**
- **ruler**
- **crayons**
- **pencil**
- **scissors**
- **glue stick**

Directions

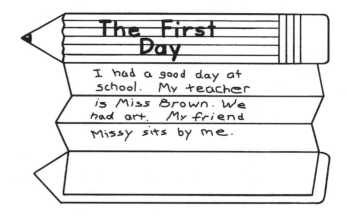

1. Trace the pencil pattern onto the yellow construction paper twice. Cut out the two pencils and add details and a title to the front cover.

2. Accordion-fold the writing paper to a 2-inch width. Glue one pencil-cover on the front and one on the back, lining them up carefully so that when the book is folded up, the pencils match exactly.

3. Open the book and write a story about your first day of school, your teacher, your schedule, or copy your homework assignment.

Bear-Shaped Book

Share a bear story of your choice with students, then encourage them to write their own original bear stories in these books.

Materials (for each book)

- 1 sheet of brown construction paper, 9 in. x 12 in. (22.5 cm x 30 cm)
- scraps of colored construction paper
- white or lined paper
- markers or crayons
- scissors
- pencil
- stapler
- patterns on pages 53–54

Directions

1. Using the pattern, trace and cut the bear from brown paper. Draw a face on the bear.

2. Using the other pattern, cut a suit for the bear, using your choice of colored-construction-paper scraps. Decorate and add a title. This will be the front cover.

3. Using the suit pattern, trace and cut several white paper pages.

4. Put the pages behind the suit-cover and staple them on the left-hand side. Print your bear story on the pages.

Pop-up Greeting Card

Here's a simple pop-up card that children will enjoy giving on any birthday occasion.

Materials (for each card)

- **1 sheet of white paper, 9 in. x 12 in. (22 cm x 30 cm)**
- **crayons**
- **copy of cake pattern on p. 55**
- **scissors**
- **scrap paper (for candles)**
- **glue stick**

Directions

1. Fold the white paper in half to make a card that is 4 1/2 in. x 6 in. and decorate the front.

2. Color and cut out the cake. Fold it down the center, colored side out, and fold the tabs back. Create candles from scrap paper and glue them onto your cake. Do *not* glue candles on the fold line.

3. Open the white card. Place the cake inside in the center, matching the two fold lines, with tabs folded underneath. Carefully glue only the tabs to the white card. The cake should fold out from the center.

4. Draw a plate under your cake and add other appropriate decorations.

5. Write a birthday greeting and be sure to sign your name!

See-Inside Book

Use this book when talking about parts of the body and their functions. You can easily either add or reduce the complexity of the project by adding or subtracting detail.

Materials (for each book)

- **3 copies of pattern on p. 56**
- **crayons, markers, or colored pencils**
- **scissors**
- **1 sheet of colored construction paper, 9 in. x 12 in. (22.5 cm x 30 cm)**
- **stapler**

Directions

1. For page 1, fold one pattern page on the fold line and add clothing, a face, hair, and so on to the body outline.

2. Carefully cut open the *top* door on the center line and along the top and bottom.

3. Fold the doors open and draw the lungs and heart on the paper that shows through the window. Turn the page and add a story under the organs. Set aside.

4. Repeat Step 1 on the next pattern page.

5. Cut open the *center* door on the center line and along the top and bottom. Fold the doors open and draw the stomach and intestines. Turn the page and add a story under the organs. Set aside.

6. Repeat Step 1 with the last pattern page.

7. Cut open the *bottom* door on the center line and along the top and bottom. Fold the doors open and draw the liver and kidneys. Add a story.

8. Stack the three folded pattern pages in order (top door, middle door, bottom door) and insert into a folded construction-paper cover. Staple together on the left-hand side. Add a title.

Hershey's Kiss-Shaped Book

Chocolate lovers will have fun describing their favorite chocolate treats inside this shape book. Any lovers of non-chocolate candy may describe other types of favorite treats.

Materials (for each book)

- **pattern on p. 57**
- **scissors**
- **2 sheets brown construction paper, 9 in. x 12 in. (22.5 cm x 30 cm) each**
- **writing paper**
- **pencil**
- **markers or crayons**
- **1 small strip of white paper**
- **glue**
- **recycled aluminum foil**
- **stapler**

Directions

1. Trace and cut the Hershey's Kiss pattern from both sheets of brown construction paper and the writing paper. Print your story on the writing paper.

2. Print the book title on the strip of white paper and glue it at the top of the front cover. Crumple and then smooth the foil and glue to the front cover. Trim around the edges, allowing some of the brown paper to show around the outside.

3. Put the story pages in order, place between the two brown Kiss shapes, and staple together on the left-hand side.

Jacket- or Shirt-Shaped Book

This book might be a good one to use when cool weather sets in and children start bundling up before leaving for school or home. Invite them to write about favorite cool-weather activities.

Materials (for each book)

- **scissors**
- **copy of pattern on p. 58**
- **2 sheets of colored construction paper, 9 in. x 12 in. (22.5 cm x 30 cm) each**
- **crayons or markers**
- **glue stick**
- **3–4 squares of white writing paper, 6 in. (15 cm) each**
- **stapler**

Directions

1. Cut out the cover pattern and trace it onto both sheets of construction paper. Carefully cut out both covers. Decorate the front cover and cut in half lengthwise to create two pieces.

2. Glue the front cover arms to the back cover arms and fold the fronts of the book open.

3. Print your story on the writing paper. Put the pages in order and staple to the back cover, across the top. Close the "jacket" and write a title on the front if you wish.

My Snowsuit
by Thomas

My mother got me the ugliest snowsuit in the world. I will not wear it. My mother can't make me.

Thomas' Snowsuit
by Robert Munsch
Annick Press 1985

Peephole Book

Encourage children to think about jobs they might enjoy as you discuss familiar community workers. Children can put themselves right into those jobs through the stories they write in this book.

Materials (for each book)

- **scissors**
- **2 sheets of colored tagboard, 9 in. x 10 in. (22.5 cm x 25 cm) each**
- **masking tape**
- **white drawing paper**
- **stapler**
- **pencil**
- **glue stick**
- **child's school photograph (or head shot you take with an instant camera)**
- **crayons or markers**

Waitress

Directions

1. To make the front cover, cut a 1-inch strip from the 10-inch side of one piece of tagboard. Turn the tagboard over and reattach the strip along the entire length with masking tape. The tape should be on the inside of the cover. This will create a hinge for easy opening.

2. Insert the desired number of pages between the tagboard covers. Staple on the left-hand side.

3. Trace or draw an oval shape on the first page and cut it out. Trace the cutout to draw on the second page an oval that lines up perfectly with the first, and cut it out. Continue the process until you can see through the entire book to the back cover.

4. Glue your photo to the back cover so that your face shows through all the holes.

5. Draw different community workers on each page. Be sure to show their uniforms and tools. Your picture face will make the community worker you!

6. Write a story to go with your illustrations or just tell your story as you turn the pages.

Computer-Shaped Book

Children will enjoy writing stories about a computer that came to life or about their experiences using the Internet in this shape book.

Materials (for each book)

- **scissors**
- **pattern on p. 59, duplicated onto white drawing paper**
- **pencil**
- **lined writing paper**
- **stapler**
- **white drawing paper**
- **glue stick**
- **utility knife (for teacher use only)**

Directions

1. Cut out the two parts of the computer pattern. Using the keyboard section as a pattern, trace and cut out several sheets of writing paper for pages. Staple the pages together near the top.

2. Assemble the computer by gluing the monitor to the keyboard where indicated on the keyboard. This will be the front cover. Trace around the entire computer on white paper and cut out. This will be the back cover.

3. Glue the two monitors together to just above the keyboard. Do *not* glue the keyboards together. Lift the top keyboard and glue the stapled pages in place between the covers. Write your story.

4. Print a title on the monitor. Practice typing your title on the keyboard cover.

Oval-Shaped Book

Here's a book you can use during a science or social studies unit. Possible story topics are numerous: recycling, pollution, explorers, oceans, continents, time zones, children around the world, and so on.

Materials (for each book)

- **scissors**
- **world map pattern on p. 60**
- **glue stick**
- **2 sheets green or blue construction paper, 9 in. x 12 in. (22.5 cm x 30 cm) each**
- **white writing paper or white drawing paper**
- **stapler**
- **pencil**

Directions

1. Cut out the world and glue it to the construction paper. Cut around the world, leaving a 1/2-inch border of construction paper around the pattern. Cut a back cover to match by tracing around the front cover.

2. Decide on a topic for your book. Cut enough oval-shaped pages from white paper to hold your story. Insert pages between the covers and staple two or three times through the center.

3. Write a story that begins on one side of the world and continues to the other. Be sure to number the pages.

Pizza Sequence Book

You may wish to make pizza in your classroom on the day you and your students create these books and stories.

Materials (for each book)

- **ruler**
- **pencil**
- **1 sheet of tan construction paper, 12 in. x 18 in. (30 cm x 45 cm)**
- **scissors**
- **crayons**
- **glue stick**
- **construction paper scraps**

Directions

1. Position the sheet of construction paper so that the long sides are the top and bottom. Using your ruler, measure and draw a vertical line through the center of the paper. Fold the outside edges in to this center line and crease so that the book opens out from the center.

2. Open the cover and use your ruler to measure and draw two horizontal lines across the inside. Now you will have six equal sections. Close the cover and do the same thing on the outside.

3. Cut the cover on the horizontal lines from the center edges to the folds.

4. Decorate the cover to look like your favorite pizza, using crayons or markers and gluing on paper scraps. Allow the glue to dry. Be sure not to glue the sections together or the book shut!

5. On the cover, number the sections 1–6. On the inside, write a sentence or two in each section to explain the sequence of making a pizza. Add illustrations, too.

People-With-Interlocking-Hands Book

This is a fun project for very young children who wish to write a bit about their families and friends.

Materials (for each book)

- scissors
- patterns on page 61
- pencil
- several pieces of construction paper (match skin color)
- markers or crayons
- ruler
- 1 Manila folder, 9 in. x 12 in.
- tape or glue stick

Directions

1. Cut out the people patterns and trace them onto construction paper. Make one for each member of your family. Color them appropriately and cut them out.

2. Print information about each family member on the back of his or her cutout. Carefully cut the slots for the interlocking hands.

3. Hold the Manila folder so that the short sides are the top and bottom. Cut the top half from the front of the Manila folder (about 6 inches). Tape or glue the bottom and bottom-right side to form a pocket. Store your family cutouts in the pocket.

4. Write family names or a short story on the front of the pocket. Add a title on the top. You may wish to add a family tree on the back.

Shape Book With Flaps

This is a good project for children who are more comfortable with single sentences than entire stories. Each sentence or fact can go in a separate compartment under a flap.

Materials (for each book)

- **markers or crayons**
- **1 sheet of white tagboard, at least 12 in. x 18 in. (30 cm x 45 cm)**
- **ruler**
- **pencil**
- **scissors**
- **glue stick or clear tape**
- **white writing paper**

Directions

1. Make a large drawing of your giant, dinosaur, or tall-tale character on tagboard and cut it out. Decide where you might place some flaps on the front. Each flap should be about about 2 inches (5 cm) square. Carefully mark the flaps with a ruler and cut them open on three sides.

2. Tape white writing paper squares behind the cut flaps. Apply tape from the back. Open the flaps and write facts about your character or a sentence from your story. Number the fronts of the flaps if it is important that they be read in order.

3. Color the character and add a title.

Halloween, Christmas, Chanukah, Valentine's Day Layered Shape Books

These shape books work as well for stories as they do for holiday greetings.

Materials (for each book)

- **2 sheets colored construction paper, 12 in. x 18 in. (30 cm x 45 cm) each**
- **ruler**
- **white writing paper**
- **scissors**
- **stapler**
- **patterns on pp. 62–65**
- **crayons**
- **markers**
- **pencil**

Directions

1. Work on a flat surface. Place the two sheets of construction paper one on top of the other. Move the top one up about 1 1/2 inches (3.5 cm). Be sure the sides remain aligned.

2. Folding the two cover sheets down from the top, fold top sheet to 1 1/2 inches (3.5 cm) above its bottom so that four 1-1/2-inch (3.5 cm) sections are visible. Make sure the sides remain aligned.

3. Insert writing paper *under* the top layer of the cover. Mark with a ruler and cut to fit. Repeat for the other three cover layers. Hold all the papers firmly in place and staple at the center top.

4. Place the selected pattern atop the layered papers and cut the book into a tree, pumpkin, heart, or dreidel shape. Restaple if necessary. Decorate the front and add a title.

5. Write a story on the writing-paper pages.

Africa-Shaped Book

Here is another project that you might offer students during the December holidays.

Materials (for each book)

- **Africa pattern on p. 66**
- **pencil**
- **white drawing paper for covers**
- **scissors**
- **red, green, and black crayons or markers**
- **writing paper**
- **stapler**

Directions

1. To make the covers, trace two Africa shapes on white drawing paper and cut them out. You may wish to decorate the covers in the colors of Kwanzaa: **black** for the color of African skin, **red** for past and present struggles, and **green** for the harvest and a prosperous future. Locate and color any country that is of special interest to you.

2. Using the Africa pattern, trace and cut out several sheets of writing paper and place them inside the covers. Staple your book together in the upper left-hand corner.

3. Write a story about Kwanzaa or research one of these topics.

   - a famous African American
   - an African proverb
   - a specific country in Africa
   - an African tribal custom
   - an animal native to Africa

Apartment-Building Book

Use this and the project that follows to encourage students to write stories about their homes and the people who live there, about their friends and neighbors, or to write about their rooms and the things they keep and do there.

Materials (for each book)

- **scissors**
- **ruler**
- **2 sheets of tagboard (for cover), 12 in. x 18 in. (30 cm x 45 cm)**
- **masking tape**
- **stapler**
- **markers**
- **white paper cut into 3 in. x 4 in. (7.5 cm x 10 cm) pieces**
- **glue stick**
- **construction-paper scraps**

Directions

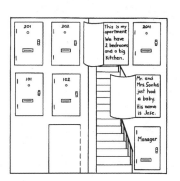

1. To make the front cover, cut a 1-inch strip from the long side of one sheet of tagboard. Turn the tagboard over and reattach the strip along the entire length with masking tape. The tape should be on the inside of the cover. This will create a hinge for easy opening.

2. Staple the front and back covers together. Decorate and cut a door in the front cover and add a title.

3. Staple the rectangles of white paper into several small books. Write and illustrate stories about the people living in the apartment building. Decorate the covers to look like doors.

4. Glue the small books in rows on the inside of the tagboard. Add a staircase, lighting, and any other details you wish inside the cover.

Single-Family House Book

Use this and the previous project to encourage students to write stories about their homes and the people who live there, about their friends and neighbors, or to write about their rooms and the things they keep and do there.

Materials (for each book)

- **markers**
- **ruler**
- **2 sheets of colored construction paper, 9 in. x 12 in. (22.5 cm x 30 cm) each**
- **scissors**
- **construction paper scraps**
- **glue stick**
- **writing paper**
- **white drawing paper**
- **stapler**

Directions

1. Design on construction paper a house-shaped cover that looks like the front of your home. Cut out your design. Be sure to include details that make your house different from others, like windows, shutters, curtains, a porch, a chimney, or bushes. Cut these items from construction-paper scraps and glue on. Print your address on the front cover.

2. Use your front cover to trace a back cover the same shape. Add details to show how the rear of your house looks.

3. Cut writing and drawing paper to fit inside the prepared covers by using one cover as a tracing pattern.

4. Write a story about the inside of your house. Include drawings and details about each room (or about your favorite rooms).

5. Put the pages in order. Staple them inside the covers along the top or the left-hand side.

Joke or Riddle Shape Book

This book could be a small-group or class project as well as a family endeavor. Encourage children to illustrate the jokes and riddles with cartoons.

Materials (for each book)

- scissors
- 2 sheets of red tagboard, 9 in. x 6 in. (22.5 cm x 15 cm) each
- patterns on pp. 67–68
- 1 sheet of white drawing paper, 9 in. x 6 in. (22.5 cm x 15 cm)
- glue stick
- several sheets of white writing paper
- pencil
- hole punch
- brass fastener
- markers

Directions

1. Cut two red tagboard covers using the cover pattern.

2. Cut big teeth from the drawing paper using the teeth pattern. Glue them to the front cover.

3. Cut the writing paper to fit inside the cover. Write your favorite jokes on the paper.

4. Punch holes in the upper left-hand corner of the cover and pages. Attach the pages and cover with a brass fastener. Print a title on the cover.

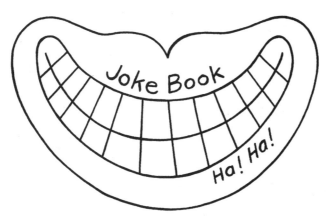

Riddle Pocket Book

Here's another project that encourages younger children to share their favorite riddles or create new ones.

Materials (for each book)

- **1 sheet of colored construction paper (for cover), 9 in. x 12 in. (22.5 cm x 30 cm)**
- **book of riddles (optional)**
- **pencil**
- **patterns on p. 69**
- **blue copier paper (for pages and pockets)**
- **red or another-color copier paper (for handkerchief inserts)**
- **scissors**
- **markers or crayons**
- **glue stick**
- **stapler**

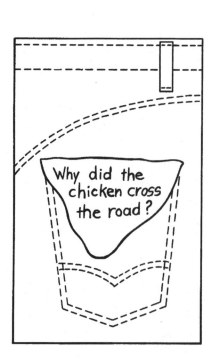

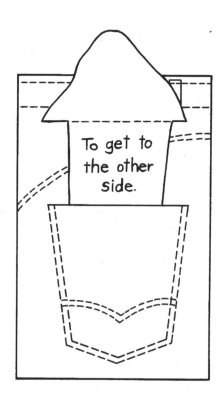

Directions

1. Fold the construction paper in half by matching the short ends. Design an interesting cover for your book of riddles.

2. Choose several riddles that you enjoy or write some original ones. Trace and cut out a pocket and a handkerchief for each one. Since each piece of blue paper will make two book pages, you will need half as many sheets of blue paper as riddles.

3. Line up the pages and fold them in half by matching the short ends. Decorate the pockets to look like blue jeans. Glue one pocket to each page along the bottom and sides of the pocket, leaving the top open.

4. Put each handkerchief in a pocket. Fold the top sections down. Print the riddles on the top sections of the handkerchiefs. Pull up each handkerchief and print the answers to the riddles on the sections that fit inside the pockets.

5. Finish decorating the pages as you wish. Assemble the finished pages and staple inside the cover along the left-hand side.

Bug-Shaped Book

Use this bug-shaped book during a science unit on insects or to inspire some original thoughts about bugs, beetles, and other critters in nature.

Materials (for each book)

- **patterns on p. 70**
- **pencil**
- **scissors**
- **2 sheets of colored construction paper, 9 in. x 12 in. (22.5 cm x 30 cm) each**
- **lined writing paper**
- **white drawing paper**
- **stapler**
- **glue stick**

Directions

1. Using the patterns, trace and cut a body and two wings from construction paper.

2. Use the wing pattern to trace and cut additional writing and drawing pages. Divide the pages into two piles that face in opposite directions, straight edges together. Place a colored wing on top of each pile.

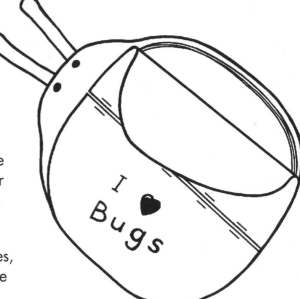

3. Staple the wings and pages onto the bug's body. Write and illustrate your story. Number the pages.

4. Finish decorating the cover of your book by gluing on cut-out spots, eyes, and antennae. Print a title. Mark one wing to show where readers should start reading your story.

Paper Wallet With Dollar Pages

This "book" makes a fun project during a math unit on money.

Materials (for each book)

- scissors
- 1 sheet of colored construction paper (laminated for durability if possible), 9 in. x 12 in. (22.5 cm x 30 cm)
- glue stick, tape, or stapler
- pencil
- several photocopies of play money (on green paper, if possible)
- 1 square of white paper, 3 in. (7.5 cm)

Directions

1. Cut a 5-inch-wide strip from the 12-inch length of the construction paper and set aside. Fold the remaining 7-inch x 9-inch rectangle in half lengthwise. Tape, or staple the short sides closed.

2. Design a coin purse from the strip you set aside. Tape or glue it in place inside the wallet on the right-hand side.

3. Print the title of your story on the white paper. Tape or glue it to the left side of the wallet like an identification card.

4. Print your story on the backs of the dollars. Be sure to number the pages. Store them inside the wallet.

Pictograph Hide Book

Share authentic Native American pictographs with students before beginning this project. Encourage students to create a series of meaningful pictographs to use for storytelling or create a set with the entire class. Be sure the books include pictograph keys so that readers can understand the stories.

Materials (for each book)

- **brown-paper grocery bag that has been soaked in water, opened at the seams, crumpled, and flattened to dry**
- **black marker or crayon**
- **hole punch**
- **1 leather shoelace or piece of yarn**
- **1 straight branch, about 1/2 in. (1.5 cm) in diameter and 10–12 in. (25–30 cm) long**

Directions

1. Tear the brown paper into rough rectangles that are approximately 9" x 11" (22.5 cm x 27.5 cm). Create a key that explains each pictograph symbol on one of these "pages."

2. Use picture writing to record your story on the remaining pages. Design a pictograph cover as well. Place the key directly under the cover.

3. Organize and stack the pages, making sure that the key is the first page. Punch a few holes in a row at the tops of all the pages at once so that the holes line up. Tie the yarn or leather to one end of the stick. Weave it through the holes and loosely around the stick. Tie off at the other end.

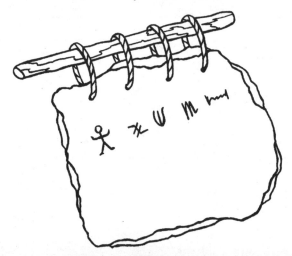

Hornbook

Children in colonial America used hornbooks in their classrooms. Recreate hornbooks with your students in connection with a study of life in the early American colonies.

Materials (for each book)

- **glue stick**
- **pattern on p. 71 (reproduced on yellow construction paper, if possible)**
- **1 sheet of tagboard, 9 in. x 12 in. (22.5 x 30 cm)**
- **scissors**
- **hole punch**
- **several sheets of writing paper, 7 in. x 8 in. (17.5 cm x 20 cm) each**
- **yarn**
- **pencil**

Directions

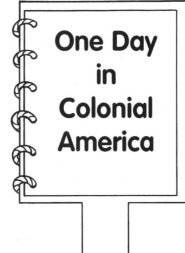

1. Glue the hornbook pattern to the tagboard. Cut out both the pattern and the tagboard at the same time. Laminate for durability.

2. Punch holes in the left side of the hornbook as marked on the pattern. Punch holes in the writing paper in the same places (place hornbook over writing paper and use holes as guides).

3. Line up the holes and use the yarn to attach the writing pages to the tag-board. Write a story about life as a settler in America. Use the information on the back page of your hornbook to check your work.

Story Quilt

This is a project that everyone in the class contributes to. Be sure to discuss with children how pioneer women used cloth scraps and worn clothing to make colorful quilts as a way of using every last bit of precious fabric. Then help children write a class story to use in this quilt project.

Materials (for each book)

- **pattern on p. 72, reproduced on colored construction paper if possible**
- **pencil**
- **markers or crayons**
- **scissors**
- **glue stick**

Directions

1. Print the words for your part of the story around the border of the quilt square. Use crayons or markers to make an illustration in the center.

2. Cut out your square.

3. Help your class glue all the squares in order on a sheet of butcher paper or on a bulletin board. Read the story.

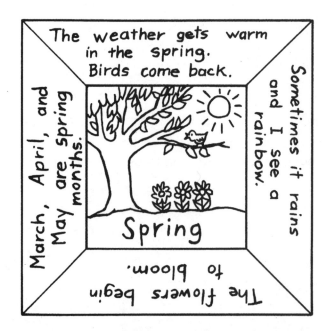

©1997 Fearon Teacher Aids

Recycling-Bin-Shaped Book

Use this project during a unit on ecology. The cover alone is a good project for younger children. Older students may write a story to go with it.

Materials (for each book)

- **5 sheets of white construction paper, 9 in. x 12 in. (22.5 cm x 30 cm) each**
- **scissors**
- **glue stick**
- **5 copies of patterns on pp. 73–74**
- **utility knife (teacher use only)**
- **construction-paper scraps for pull-out sections**
- **crayons or markers**
- **2 sheets of cardboard from grocery packaging, 10 in. x 7 in. (25 cm x 17.5 cm) each**
- **hole punch**
- **looseleaf ring**

(Directions continued on following page)

Directions

1. Fold each sheet of construction paper in half by matching the short sides. Each folded sheet will be *one* page of your book. The folds will go on the outside, as the pages are double-faced.

2. Cut out and glue recycling bins on the fronts of four of the pages. Cut out and glue the trash can on the fifth page. Carefully cut open the slots as marked in the top of each pattern or get help from your teacher.

3. Cut out the pull-out sections. Gently fold the pull-out sections and insert them into the slots.

4. Glue the open edges of each page closed. Label the bins *Paper*, *Glass*, *Aluminum*, and *Plastic*, and the can *Trash*. Pull up the inserts and draw appropriate items to be recycled in each bin. Draw things that are *not* recyclable on the trash-can pull-out.

5. Glue a collage of labels, foil, and wrappers on your cardboard front cover. Print a title.

6. Finish by writing a story about recycling. Punch holes in the upper-left corner of the cover and pages and bind with a looseleaf ring.

Cereal-Box Book

This project works well as a robot or as any sort of invention or machine that children wish to design and write about.

Materials (for each book)

- **scissors**
- **ruler**
- **1 medium-sized cereal box, empty**
- **masking tape**
- **aluminum foil**
- **brass fasteners**
- **cardboard tubes**
- **clear tape**
- **buttons**
- **bottle caps**
- **pipe cleaners**
- **glue stick**
- **pencil**
- **several sheets of lined writing paper, 8 1/2 in. x 5 1/2 in. (20 cm x 13 cm) each**
- **drawing paper**
- **stapler**

(Directions continued on following page)

Directions

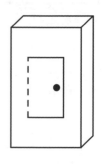

1. Carefully cut a 5 1/2" x 8 1/2" x 5 1/2" three-sided opening in the back of the box, leaving the left side attached, like a door. Fold the door open.

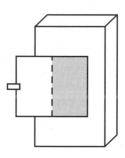

2. Tape the top and bottom of the box securely with masking tape. Cover the entire surface with aluminum foil. The door in the back should open and close freely. Attach a brass fastener to act as a knob that will either hold the door closed or release it when rotated.

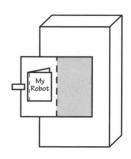

3. Design a robot using a variety of art supplies. Cover cardboard tubes with foil and tape in place for arms. Buttons and bottle caps may become eyes and knobs. Add spiral wires made from pipe cleaners.

4. Write a story about your robot. If you wish, include drawings of its inner workings. Put the pages in order. Open the door in the robot's back and staple the story pages to the door down the left-hand side.

©1997 Fearon Teacher Aids

Sneaker-Shaped Book

Children design their own covers for this project. Encourage them to design a great new sneaker and to write a story about what happens to the wearers of these terrific shoes.

Materials (for each book)

- **markers or crayons**
- **2 sheets of colored construction paper, 9 in. x 12 in. (22.5 cm x 30 cm)**
- **hole punch**
- **scissors**
- **several sheets of lined writing paper**
- **pencil**
- **1 shoelace**

Directions

1. Draw your sneaker on one sheet of construction paper. Be sure to punch at least two holes for the shoelace to go through. Decorate the sneaker to use as a cover. Cut out your sneaker and use it as a pattern to trace and cut out a back cover from the other sheet of construction paper. Punch holes to match those in the front cover.

2. Use your sneaker cover to trace and cut writing pages to match. Punch holes to match the holes in the cover.

3. Write a story about what happens when you put on these nifty sneakers.

4. Line up the pages, place one cover on top and the other on the bottom, and tie them together at the top with the shoelace.

Select-a-Sport Book

Students write about a sport they like to play or watch in this book project with two rotating wheels on the cover.

Materials (for each book)

- **patterns on pp. 75–76**
- **glue stick**
- **2 tagboard squares, 7 in. (17.5 cm) each**
- **scissors**
- **crayons**
- **2 brass fasteners**
- **pencil**
- **several writing paper squares, 7 in. (17.5 cm) each**
- **hole punch**
- **2 looseleaf rings or yarn**

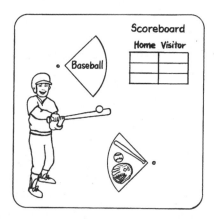

Directions

1. Use the patterns to make two tagboard circles. Glue the cover pattern to one piece of tagboard and carefully cut out the wedges or ask your teacher for help. Trim away excess tagboard around the edges. Use the front cover as a pattern to make a back cover from the other tagboard square.

2. Choose a sport that you enjoy playing or watching. Add a uniform and color the athlete on the cover to look like he or she is playing that sport.

3. Fill in the scoreboard with information about a game you have seen or in which you have played.

4. Poke holes through the wheels and front cover where indicated and attach the wheels behind the front cover with paper fasteners.

5. Write a story about the game, using lots of details to describe the action.

6. Assemble all the pages between the covers. Punch holes as marked through both covers and the finished pages. Attach with looseleaf rings or yarn.

Train-Shaped Book

Students spin the wheels on the train to find story prompts to spark their transportation stories. Blank wheels are included with the patterns so that you and your students may create your own prompts.

Materials (for each book)

- **scissors**
- **patterns on pp. 77–78, duplicated on colored paper if possible**
- **crayons or markers**
- **hole punch**
- **3 brass fasteners**
- **colored construction paper**
- **writing paper**
- **stapler**

Directions

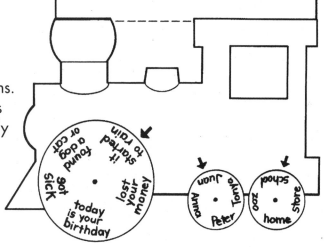

1. Cut out the train and wheel patterns. Color the train and punch holes as indicated. Attach the wheels loosely with brass fasteners. Be sure they will spin easily. Draw on the train small arrows that point to each wheel. You will use the character, setting, and problem to which the arrows point for your story.

2. Using the train shape, trace and cut a back cover and writing papers.

3. Spin each wheel one time. Create a story using the character, setting, and problem that the arrows point to. Include yourself as a main character and think of a good solution to end the story.

4. Organize your finished pages inside the covers and staple across the top.

©1997 Fearon Teacher Aids

Folding Postcard Book

Encourage students to tell about real or imaginary journeys as they write the postcards for this book.

Materials (for each book)

- **pencil**
- **4 sheets of lightweight white tagboard, 5 in. x 8 in. (12.5 cm x 20 cm) each**
- **markers**
- **clear tape**

Directions

1. Choose a place you have visited or a place you would like to visit. Write three postcards to real or imaginary friends or relatives. Tell about what you have seen and done.

2. Address the cards correctly. Design a postage stamp for each card.

3. Make colorful drawings of important landmarks or tourist sites on the fronts of the cards.

4. Tape the backs of the cards together along the 5-inch sides to make an accordion-fold book. Make a cover for your book and give it a title.

Television-Shaped Book

Children will enjoy recounting episodes from their favorite TV shows in this shape book. They might even wish to write an episode of their own.

Materials

- **pattern on p. 79**
- **pencil**
- **scissors**
- **2 squares of colored tagboard, 9 in. (22.5 cm) each crayons or markers**
- **several squares of white writing paper, 8 1/2 in. (22 cm) each**
- **hole punch**
- **2 looseleaf rings (or yarn)**

Directions

1. Using the pattern, trace and cut a "screen" from the center of one piece of tagboard. This will be the front cover. Decorate the rest of the cover to look like a TV. Laminate.

2. Draw a picture and design a title page for your favorite television show. Check to be sure it will show through the opening in the cover.

3. Write a story recalling an episode of the show that you remember well. You may wish to retell the story like a play, writing dialogue, or you may wish to create a new episode starring your favorite character(s).

4. Assemble the pages in order. Align them within the covers and punch two holes at the top. Attach with looseleaf rings.

Changeable-Weather Book

This is a great project to use during a science unit on weather or as the seasons are changing. Encourage young children to create simple stories about weather-related activities.

Materials (for each book)

- **scissors**
- **2 squares of colored tagboard, 9 in. (22.5 cm) each**
- **masking tape**
- **several squares of white drawing paper, 8 in. (20 cm) each**
- **pencil**
- **crayons or markers**
- **several squares of laminating plastic, 8 in. (20 cm) each**
- **stapler**
- **glue stick**
- **construction paper scraps**

Directions

1. Cut a 1-inch strip from the 9-inch length of one piece of tagboard. Turn the tagboard over and reattach the strip along the entire length with masking tape. The tape should be on the inside of the cover. This will create a hinge for easy opening.

2. On white paper, write a story that includes several changes in the weather. Add simple pictures.

3. To create overlays for your pictures, lay the plastic over the finished pictures. Staple at the left edge to hold in place. Glue cut-paper pieces in appropriate places to change the weather scene.

4. Design a cover and add a title. Organize the pages and staple them into the covers.

Child
(cut 1)

Pencil
(cut 1)

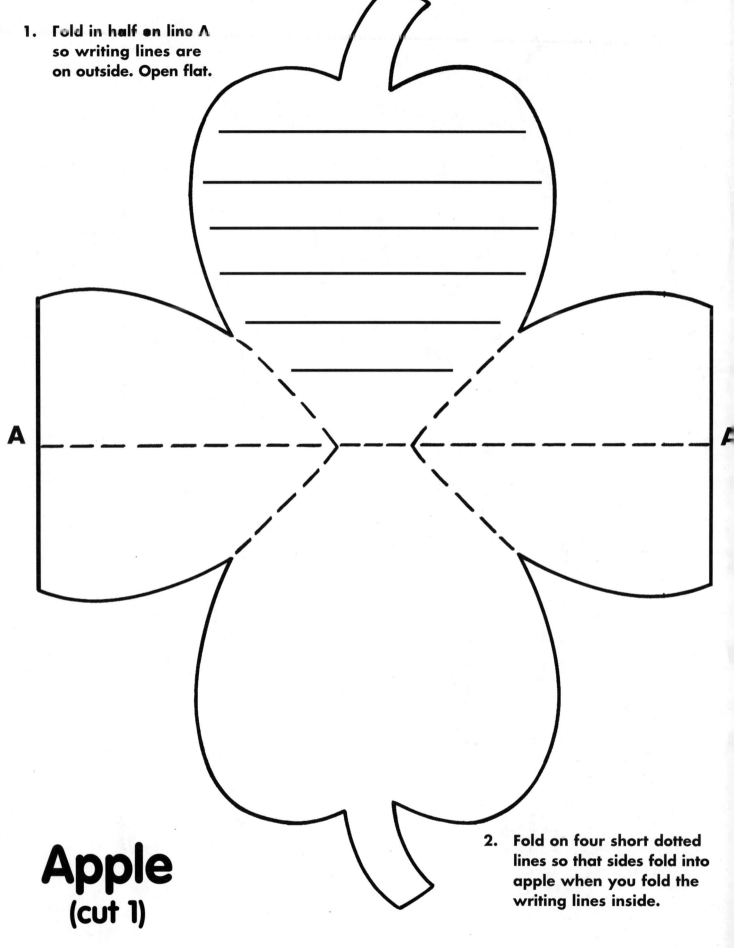

1. Fold in half on line A so writing lines are on outside. Open flat.

2. Fold on four short dotted lines so that sides fold into apple when you fold the writing lines inside.

Apple
(cut 1)

A

A

Backpack
(cut 1)

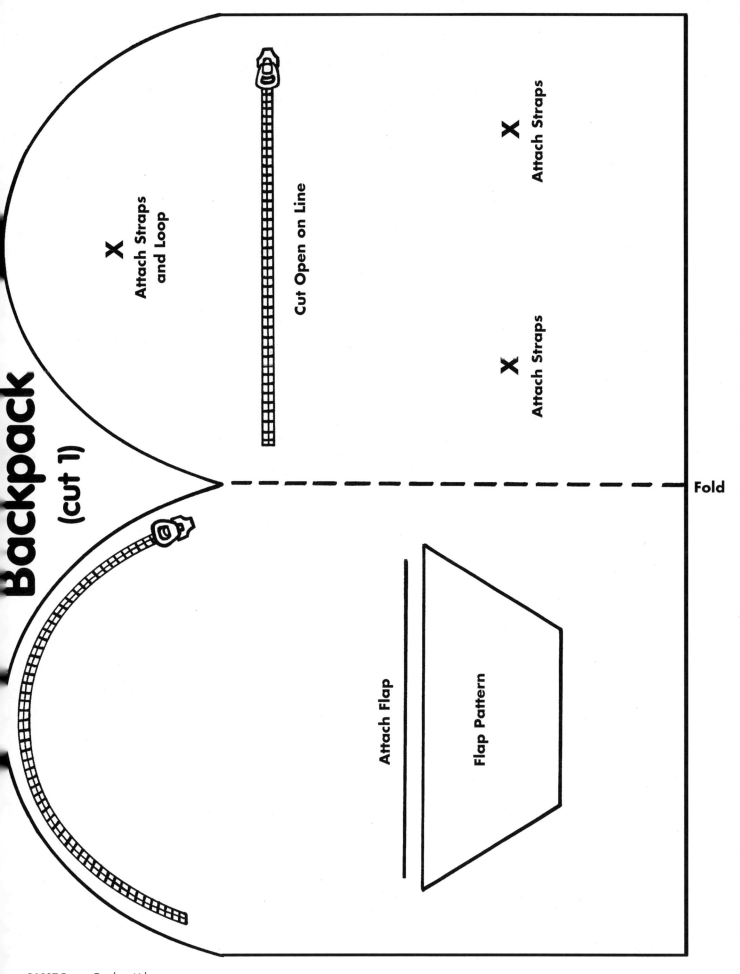

X
**Attach Straps
and Loop**

Cut Open on Line

X
Attach Straps

X
Attach Straps

Fold

Attach Flap

Flap Pattern

Crayon Box

(photocopy 8)

Bear
(cut 1)

Bear Suit
(cut 1)

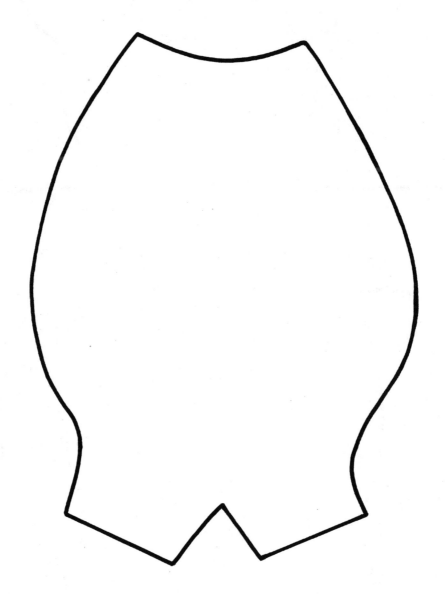

Birthday Cake
(cut 1)

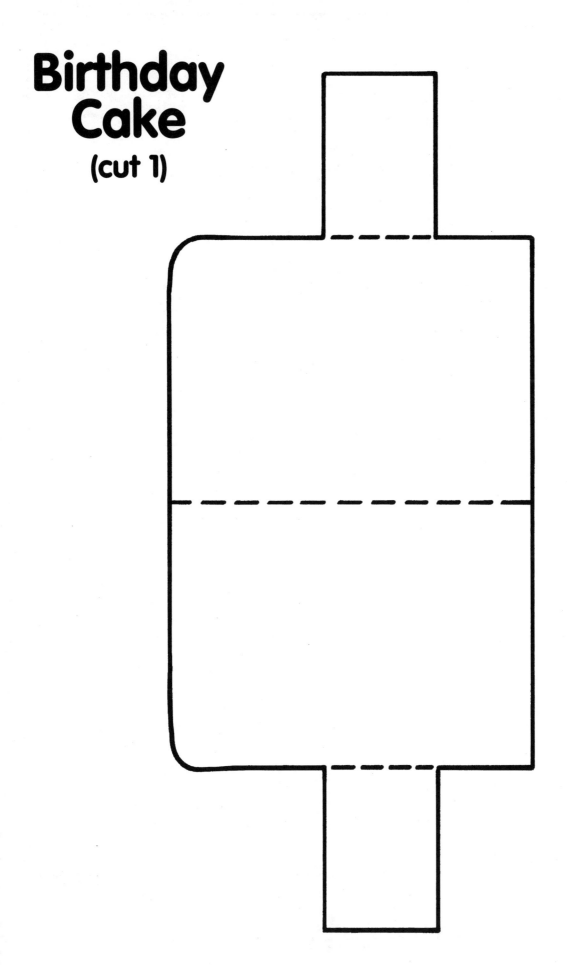

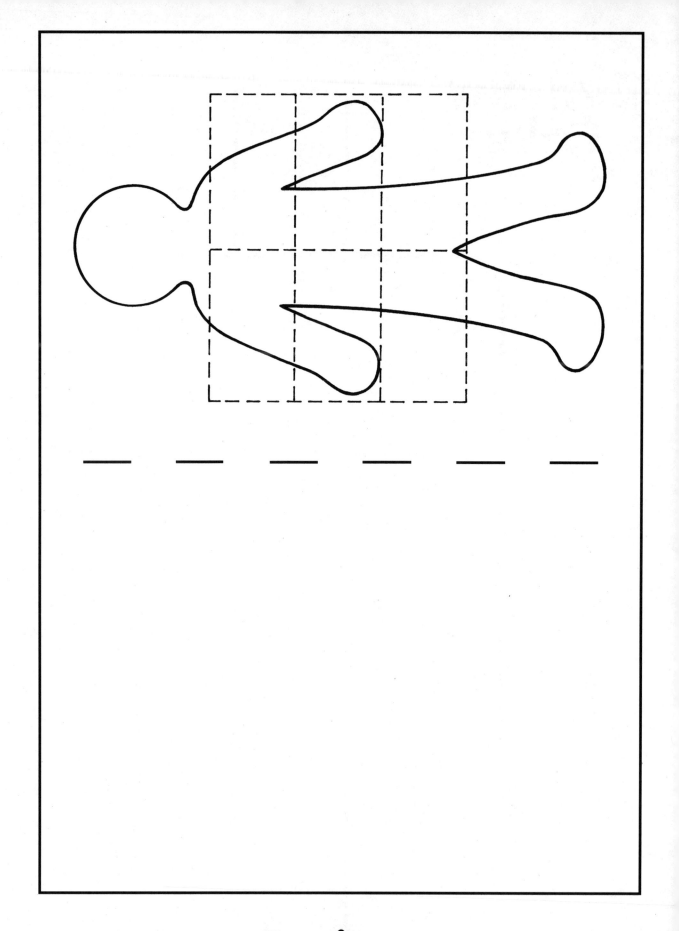

Body
(photocopy 3)

Hershey's Kiss

(cut 2)

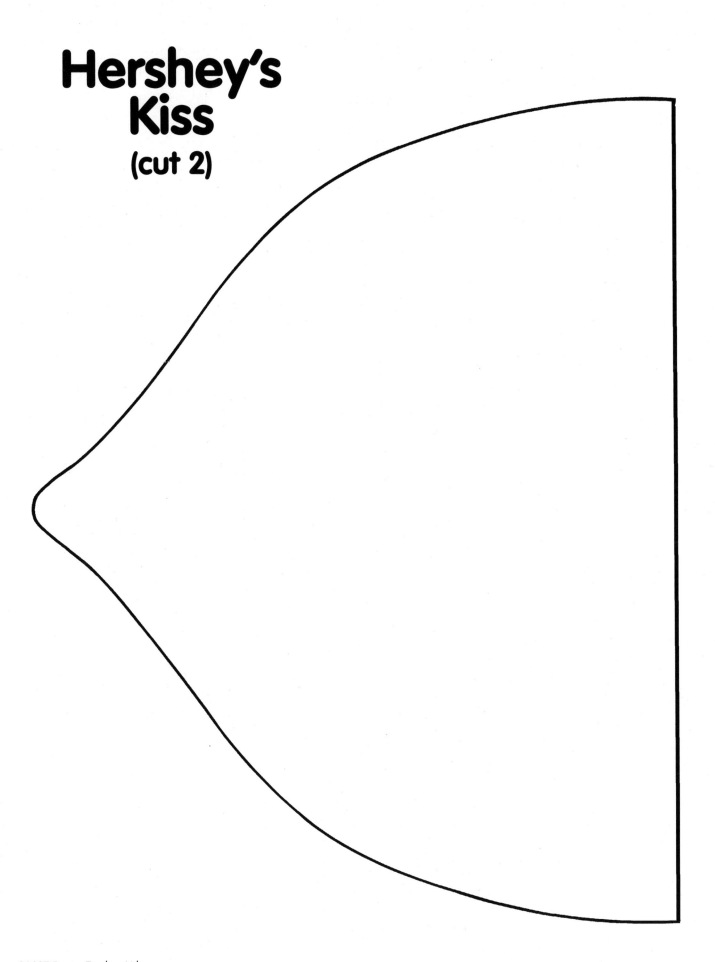

Jacket
(cut 2)

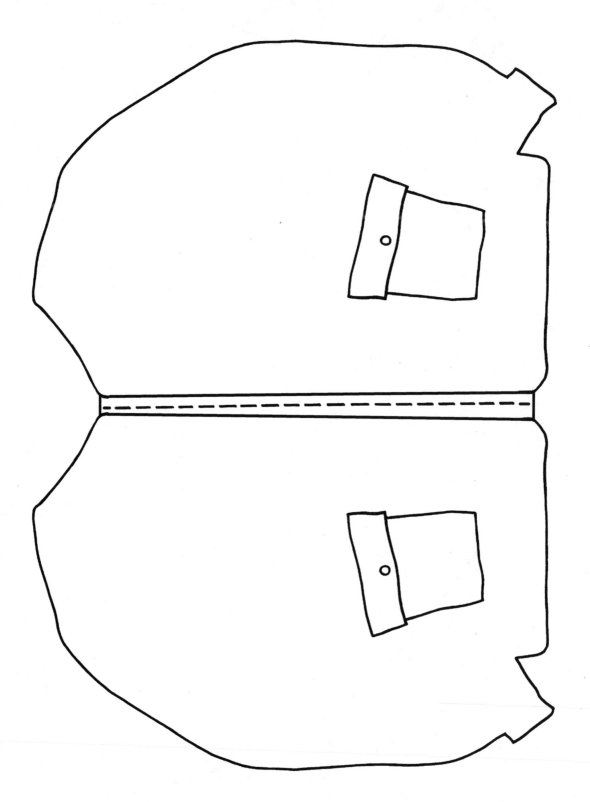

Computer Monitor
(cut 1)

Keyboard
(cut 1)

Earth
(cut 1)

Families
(cut as needed)

Chanukah
(cut 1)

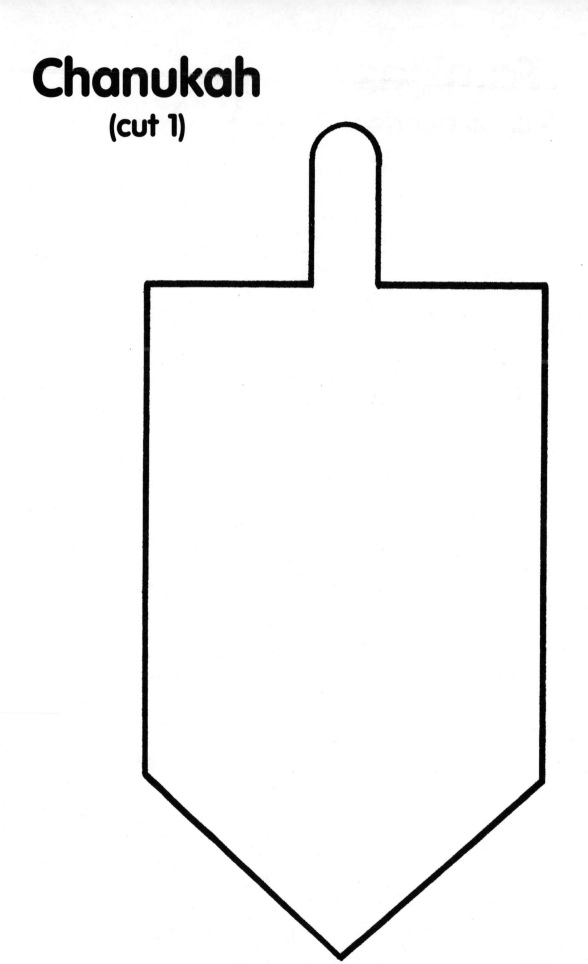

Christmas
(cut 1)

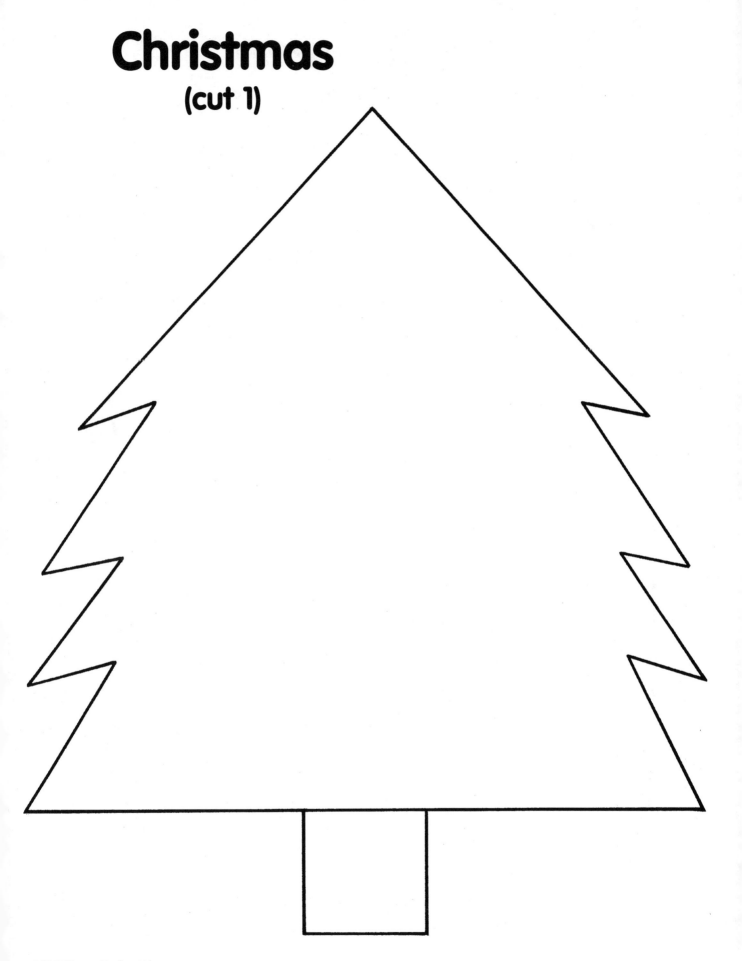

Halloween
(cut 1)

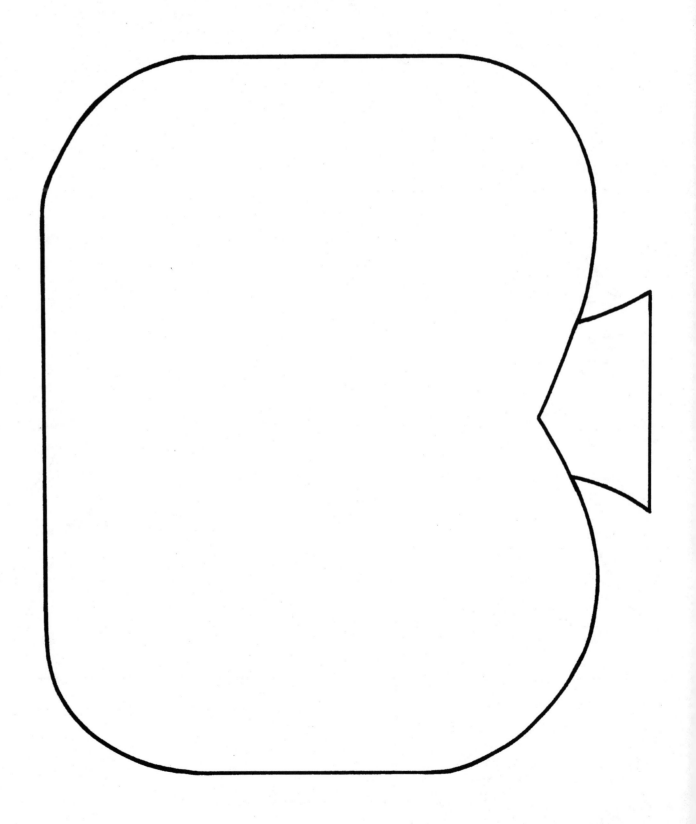

Valentine's Day
(cut 1)

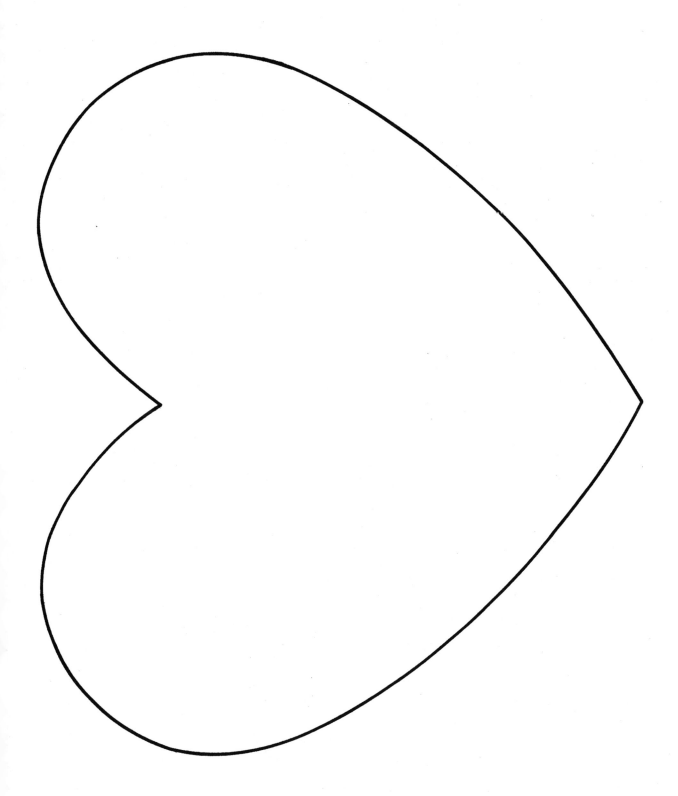

Kwanzaa
(cut 1)

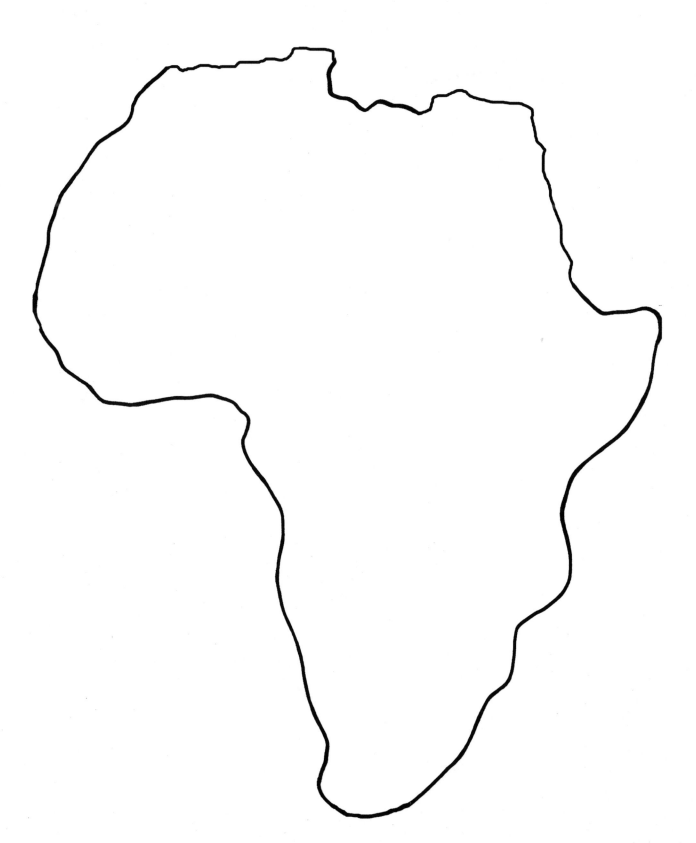

Lips
(cut 2)

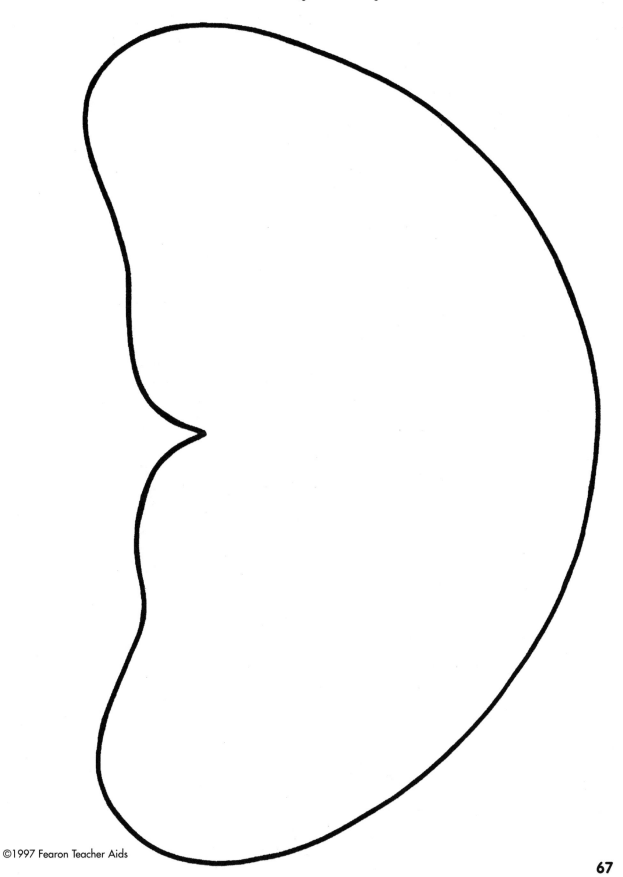

Teeth
(cut 1)

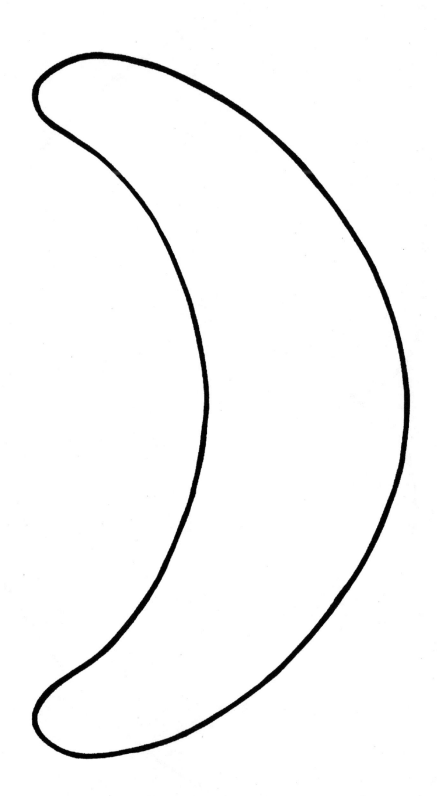

Pocket
(cut as needed)

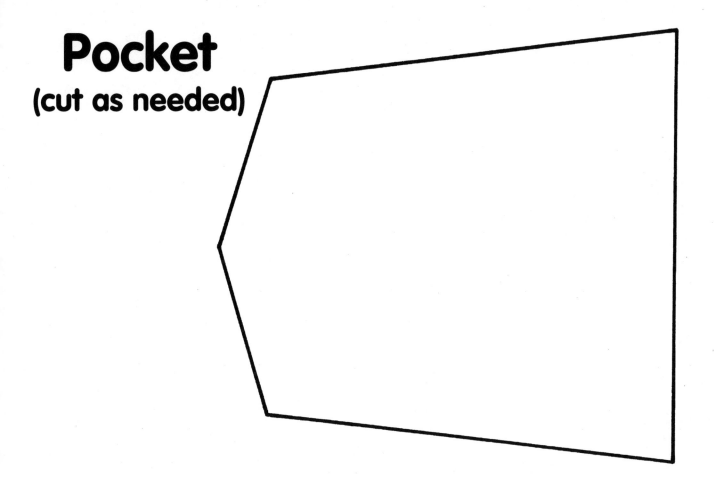

Handkerchief
(cut as needed)

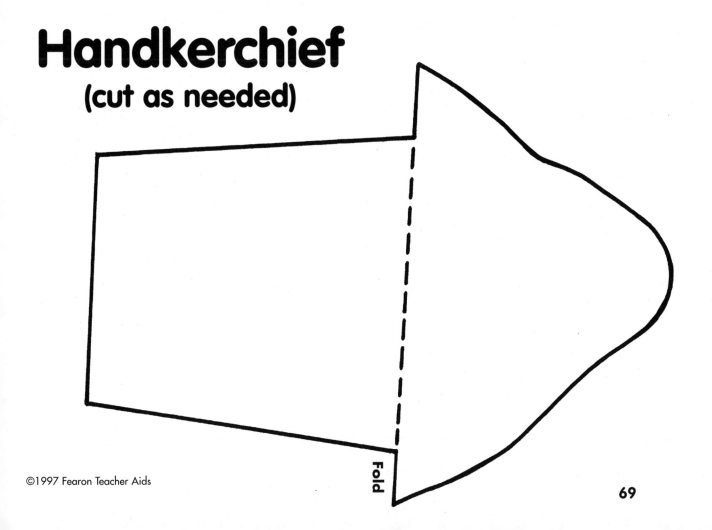

Fold

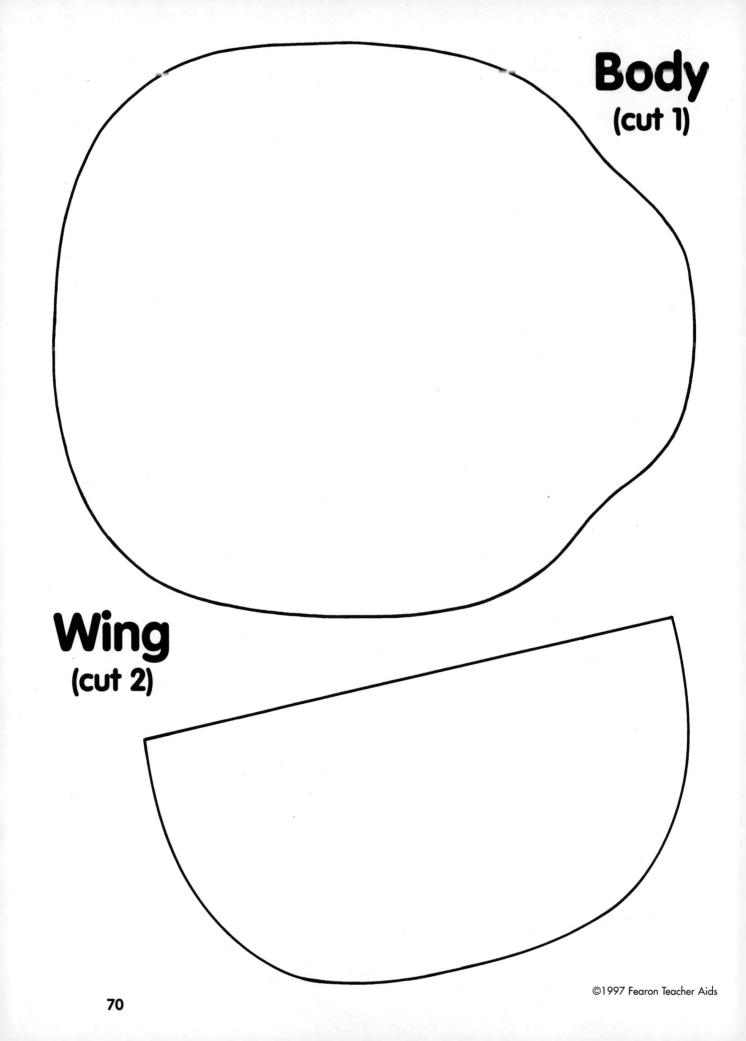

Body
(cut 1)

Wing
(cut 2)

Aa Bb Cc Dd Ee Ff Gg Hh Ii
Jj Kk Ll Mm Nn Oo Pp Qq Rr
Ss Tt Uu Vv Ww Xx Yy Zz

bat	late
bet	creep
bit	bite
pot	hole
cup	cure

Hornbook
(photocopy 1)

Quilt Square
(cut 1)

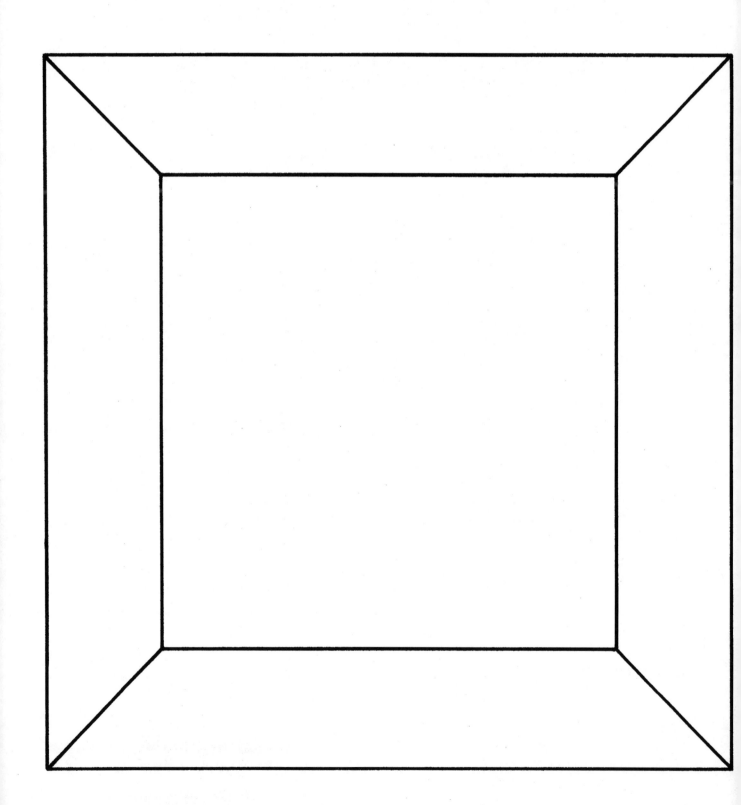

Trash Can
(cut 1)

Recycling Bin
(cut 4)

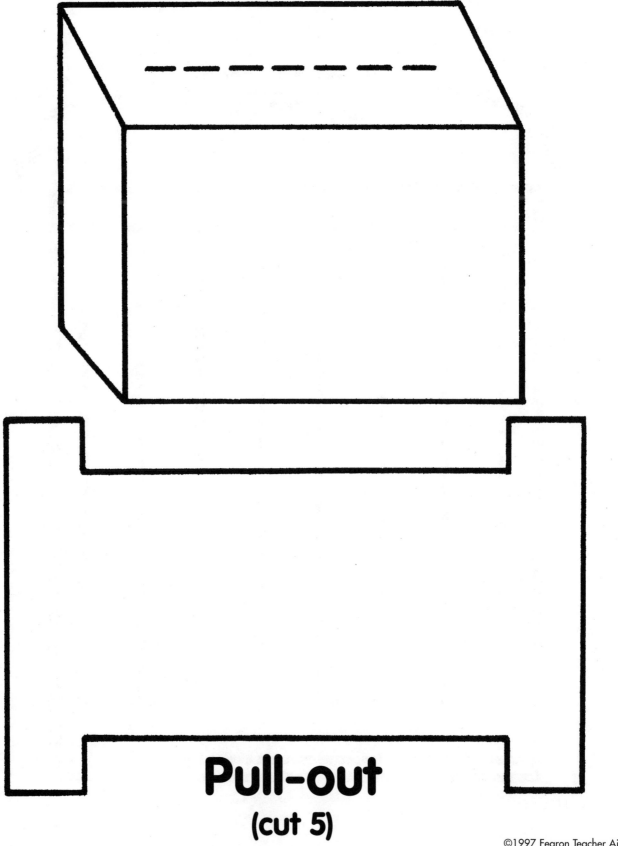

Pull-out
(cut 5)

Sports
(cut 1)

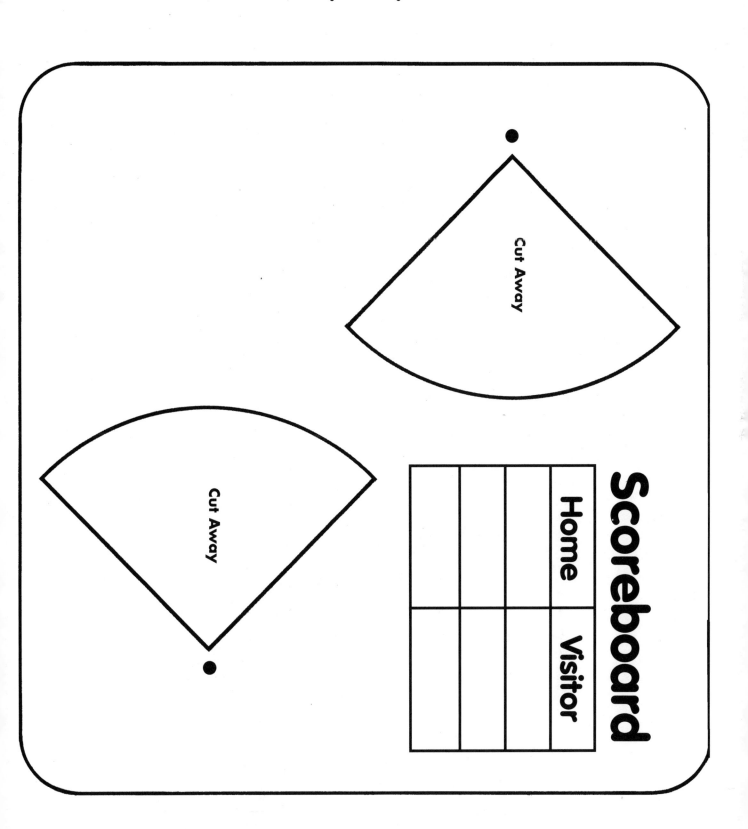

Cut Away

Cut Away

Scoreboard

Home	Visitor

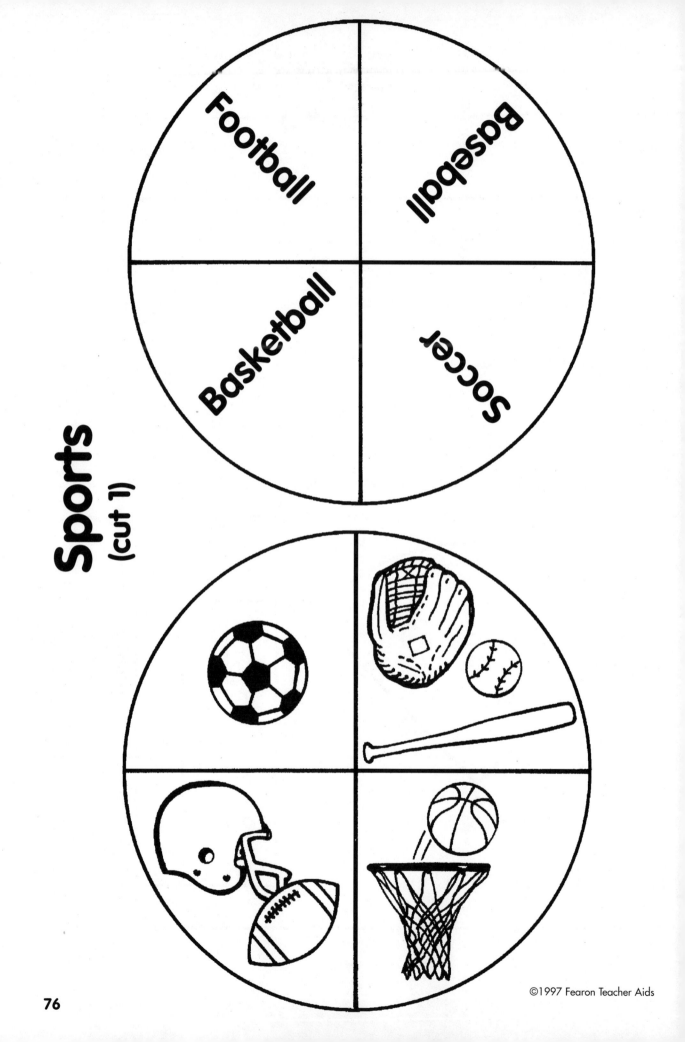

Sports
(cut 1)

Transportation
(cut 1)

Transportation Wheels

Problem Wheel

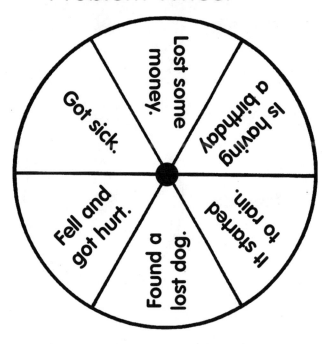 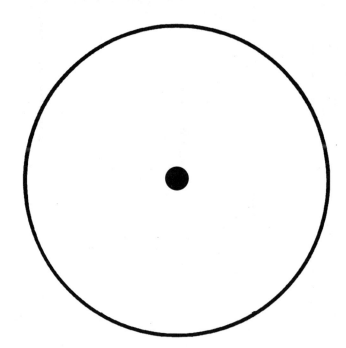

Character Wheel

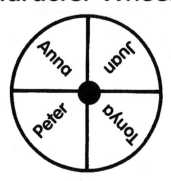 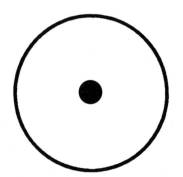

Setting Wheel

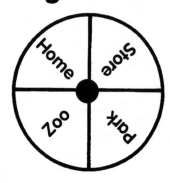 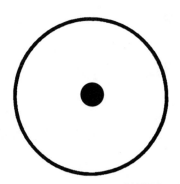

TV Screen
(cut 1)

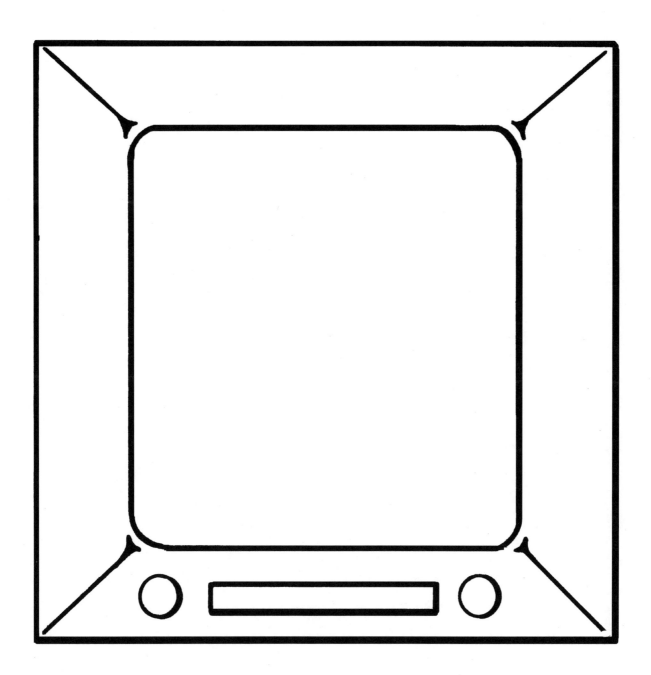